Damone's Abstract Coloring Book

volume 5

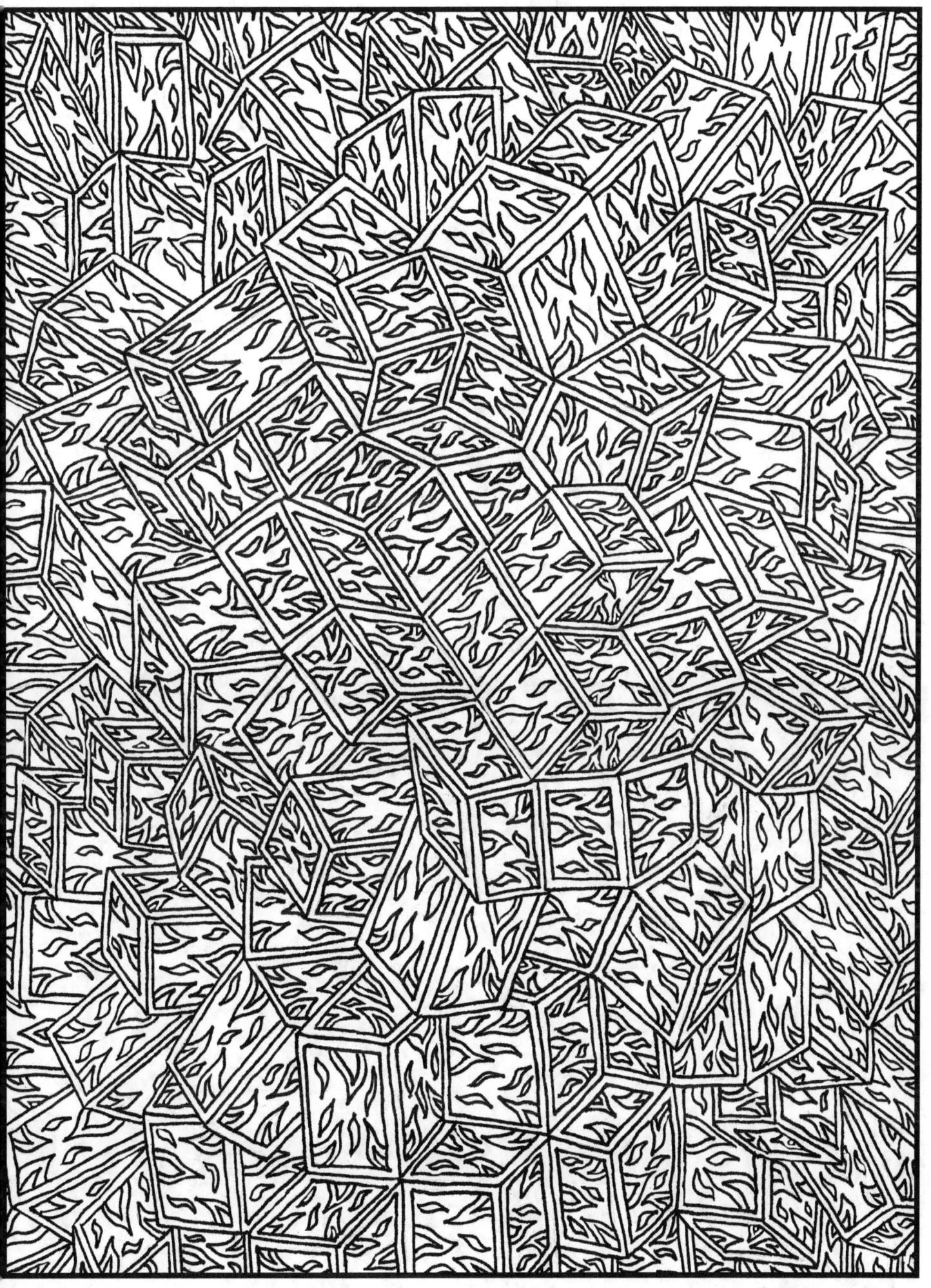

© Damone Heins

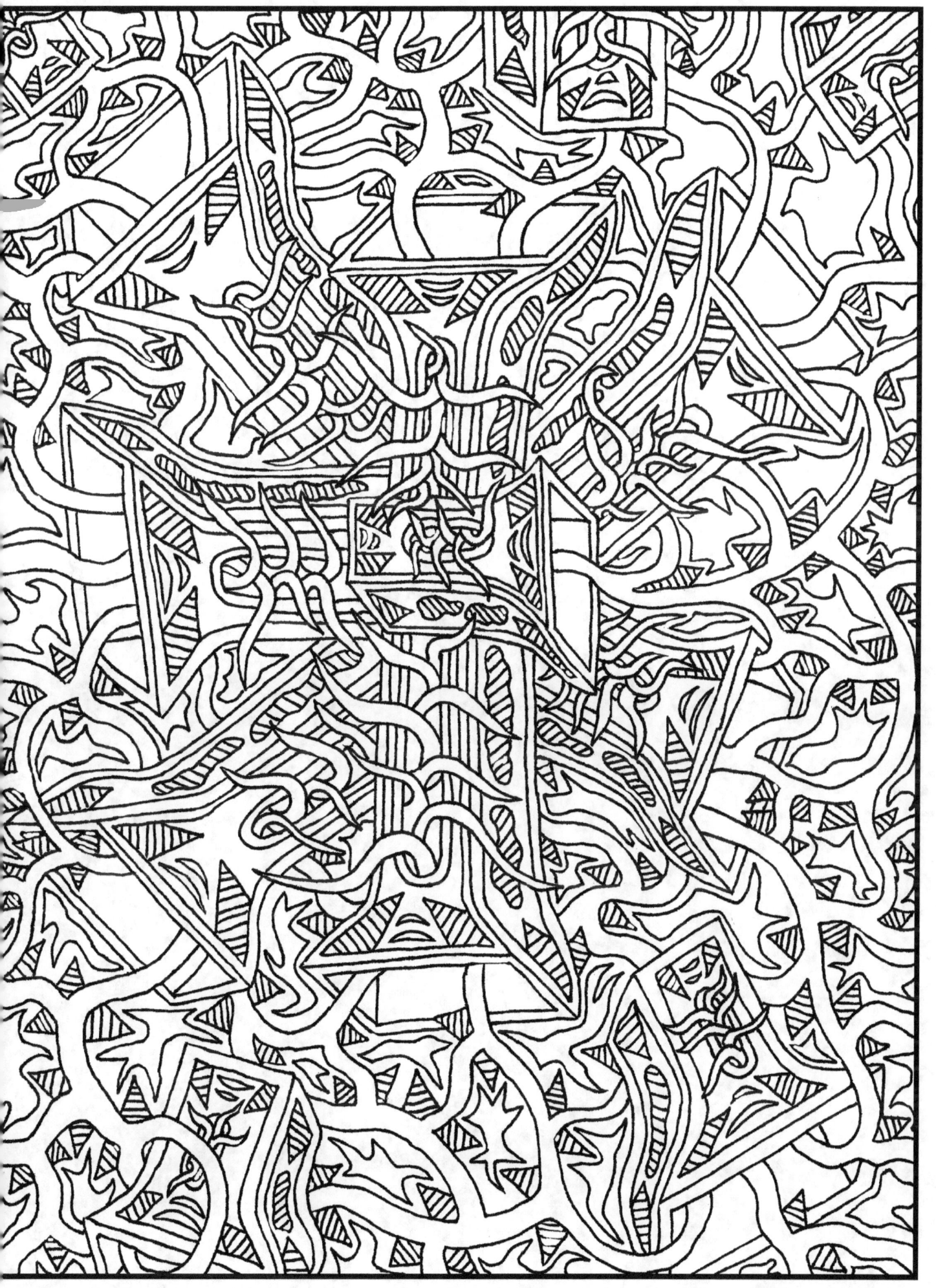

© Damone Heins

© Damone Heins

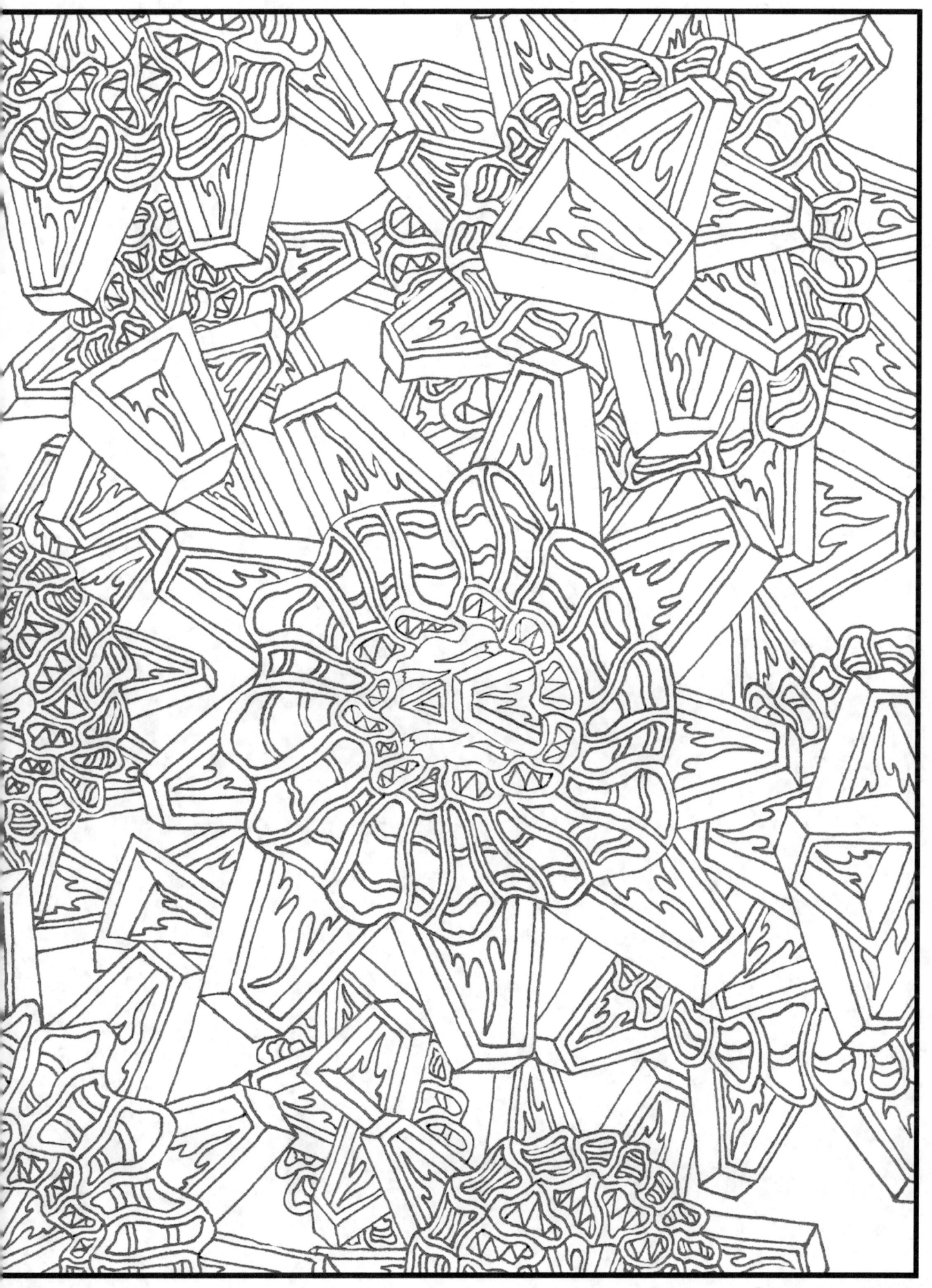

© Damone Heins

© Damone Heins

© Damone Heins

© Damone Heins

© Damone Heins

© Damone Heins

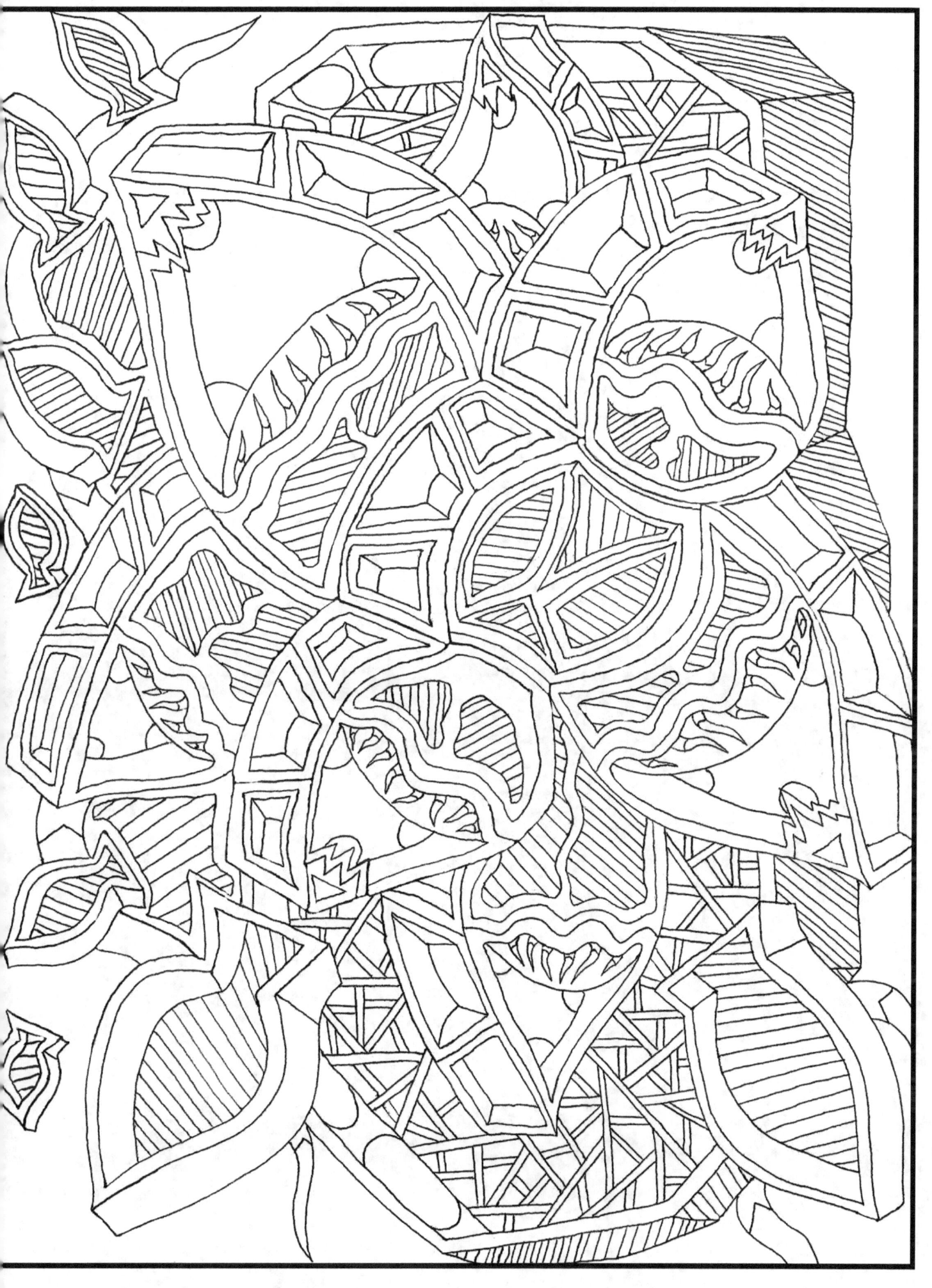

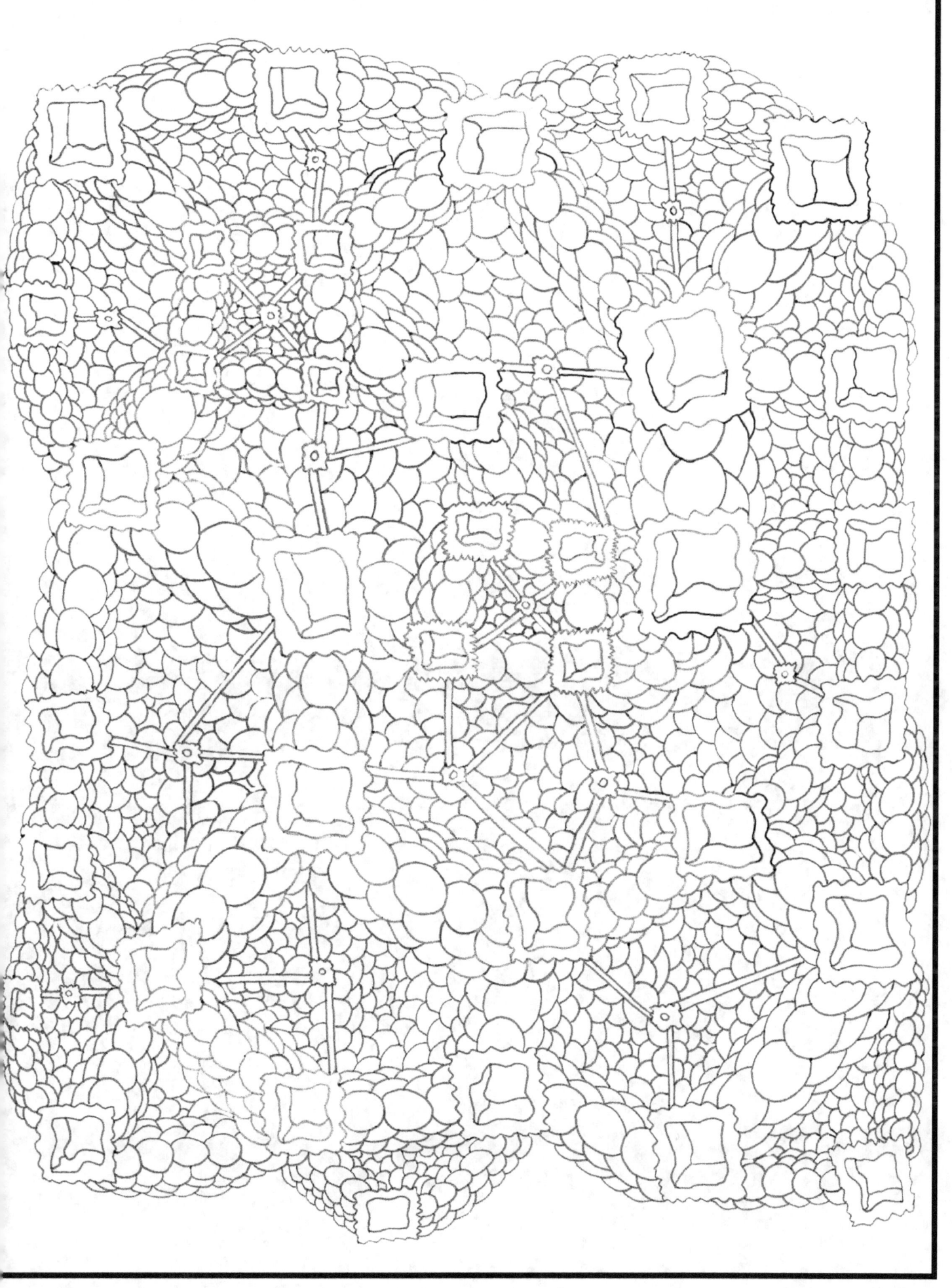

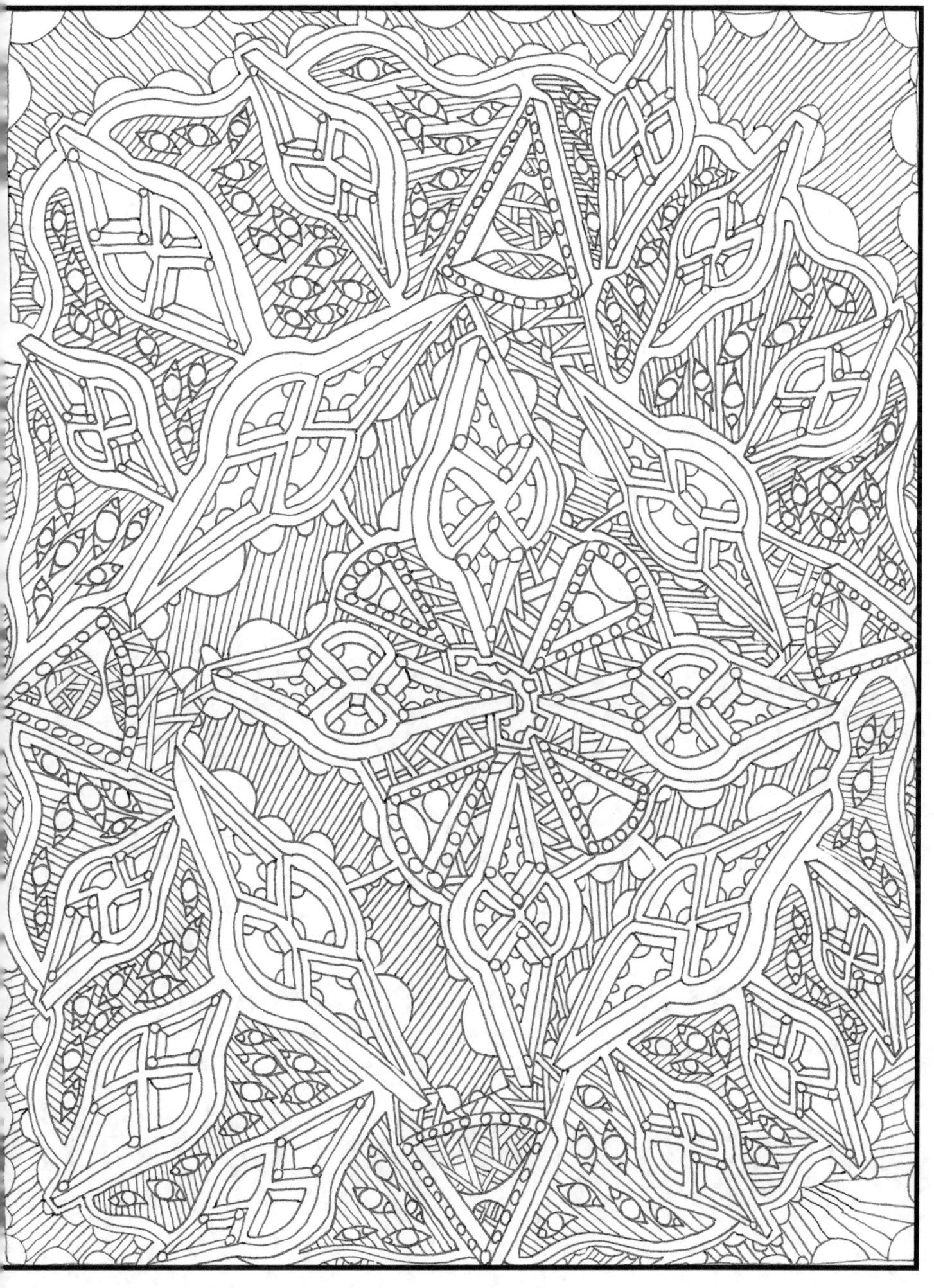

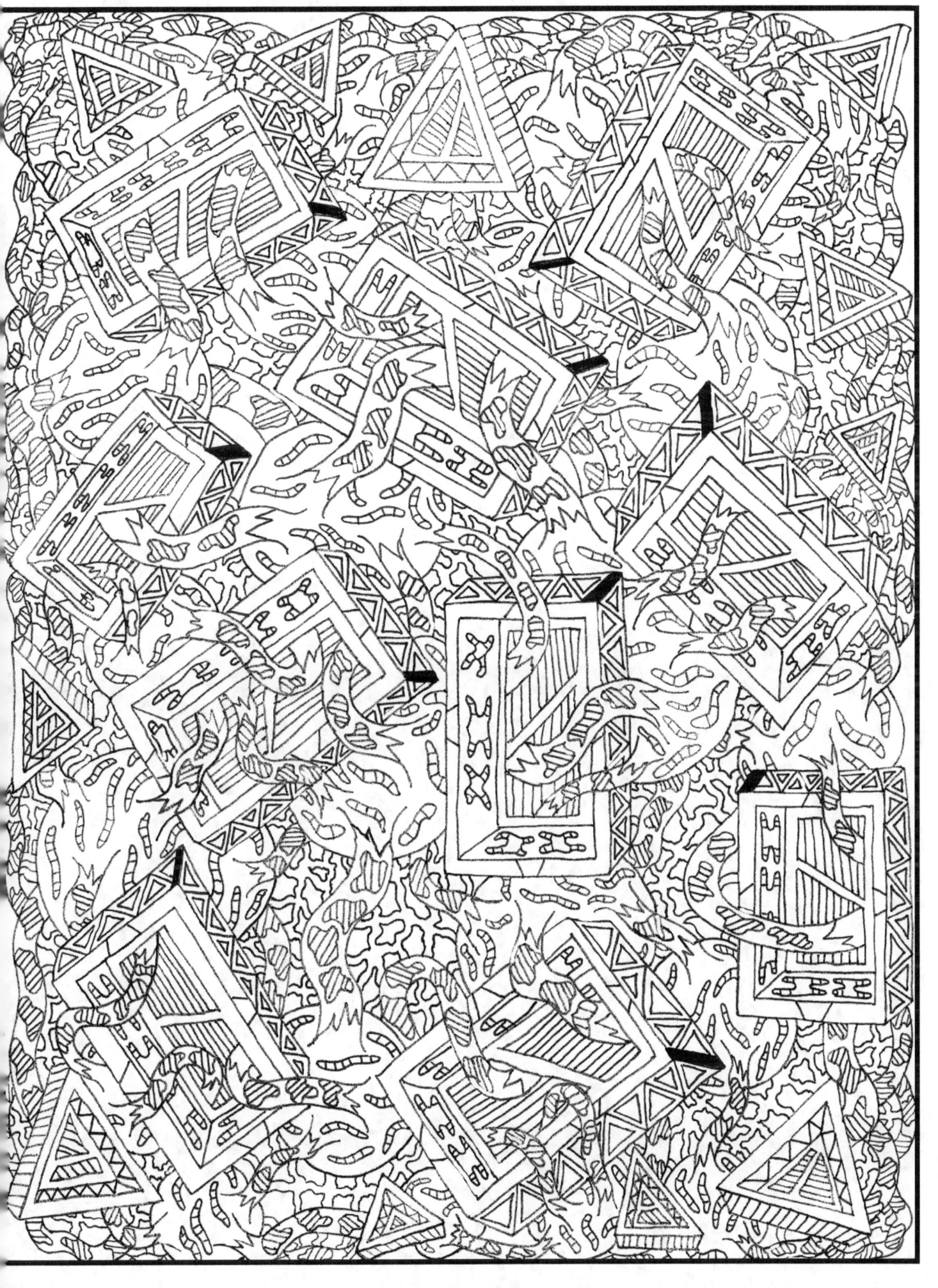

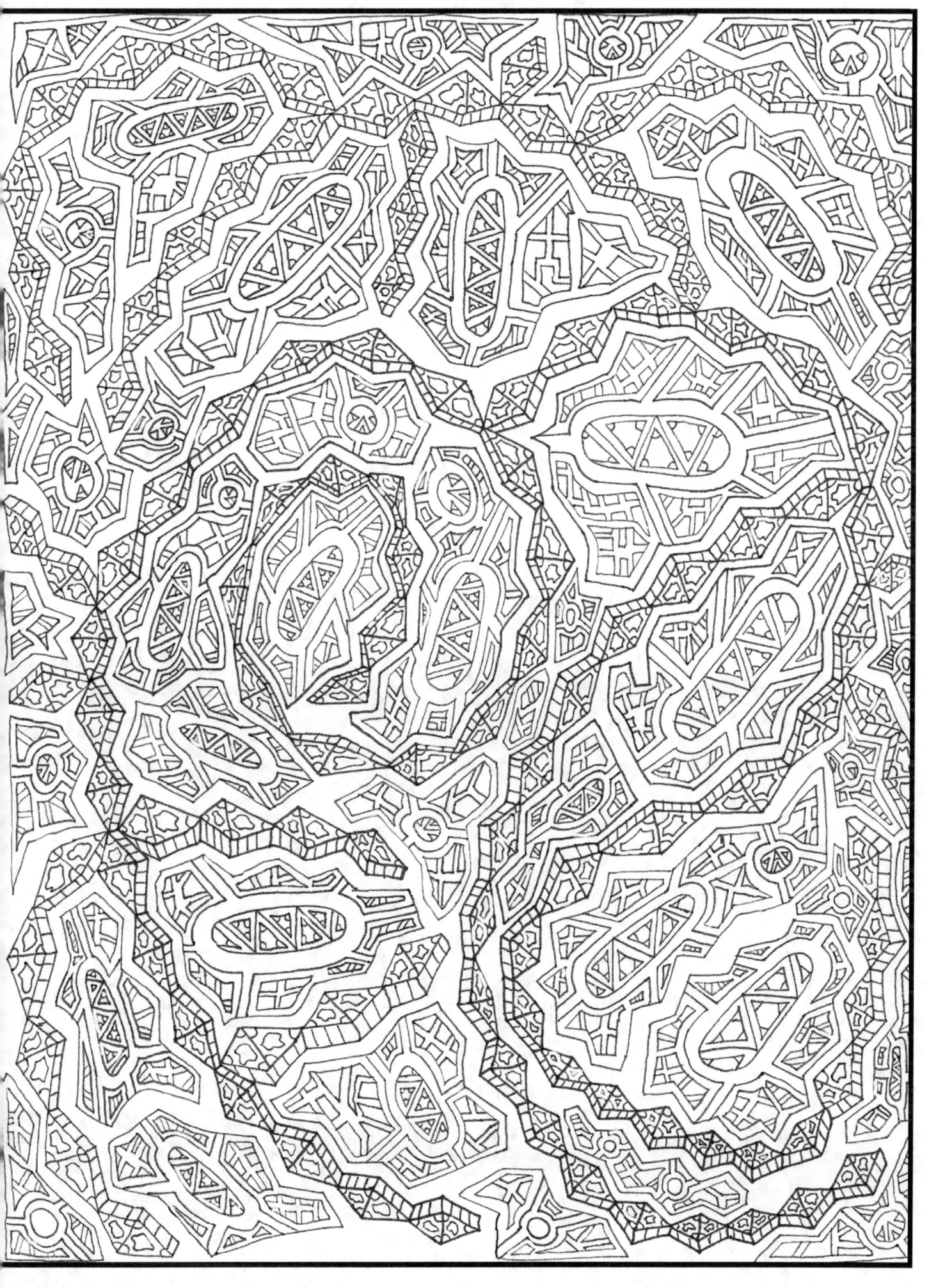

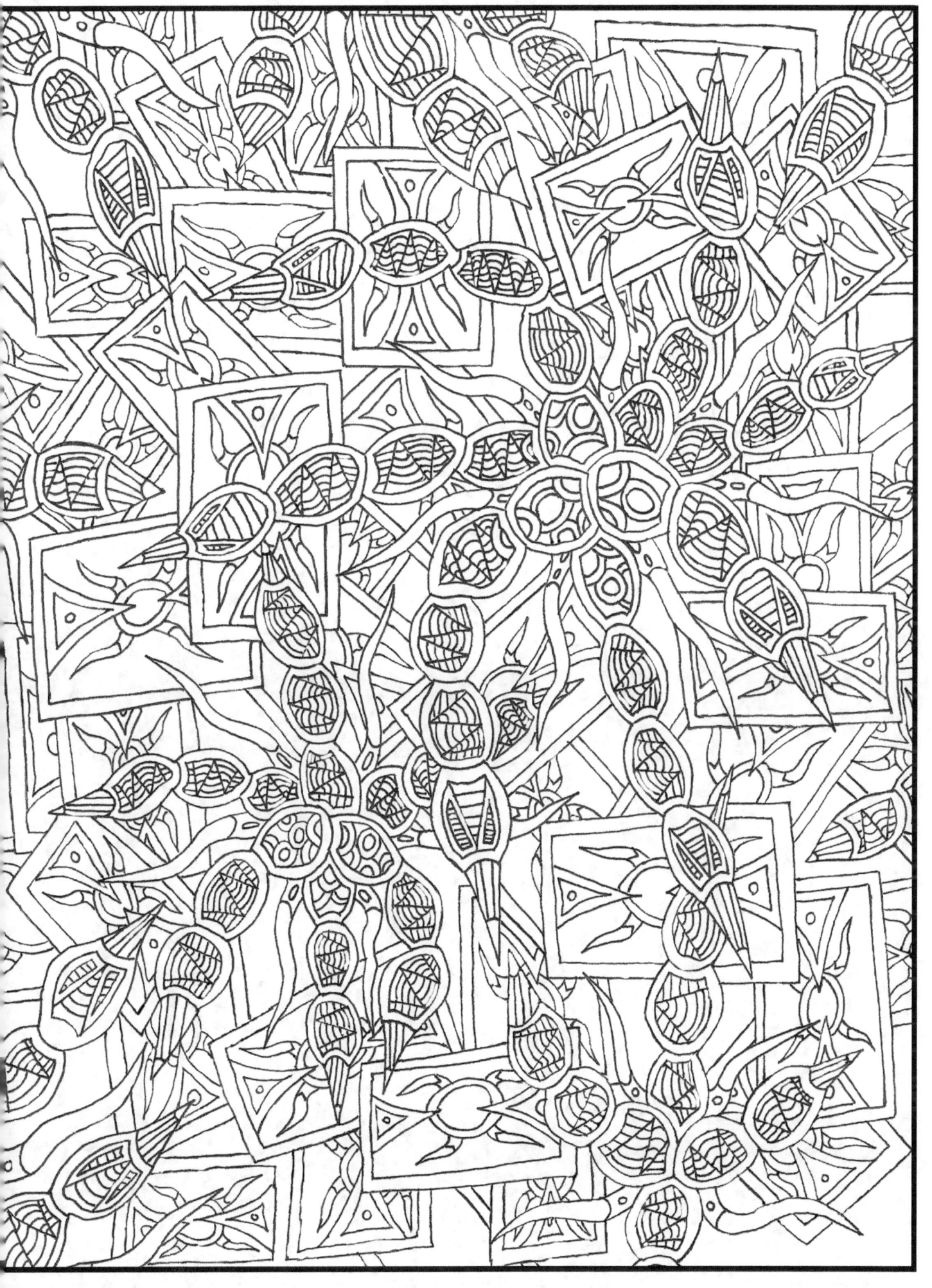

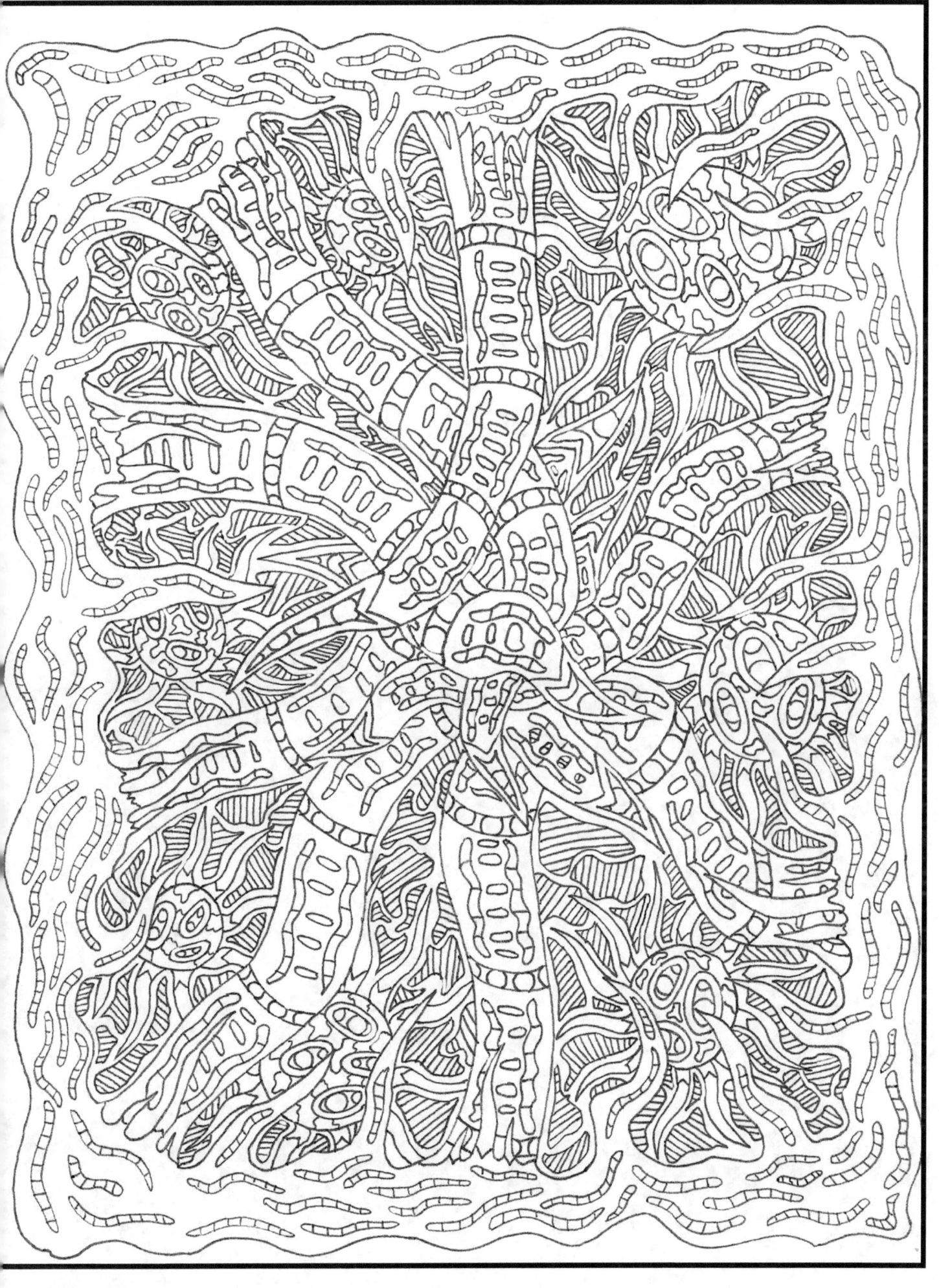

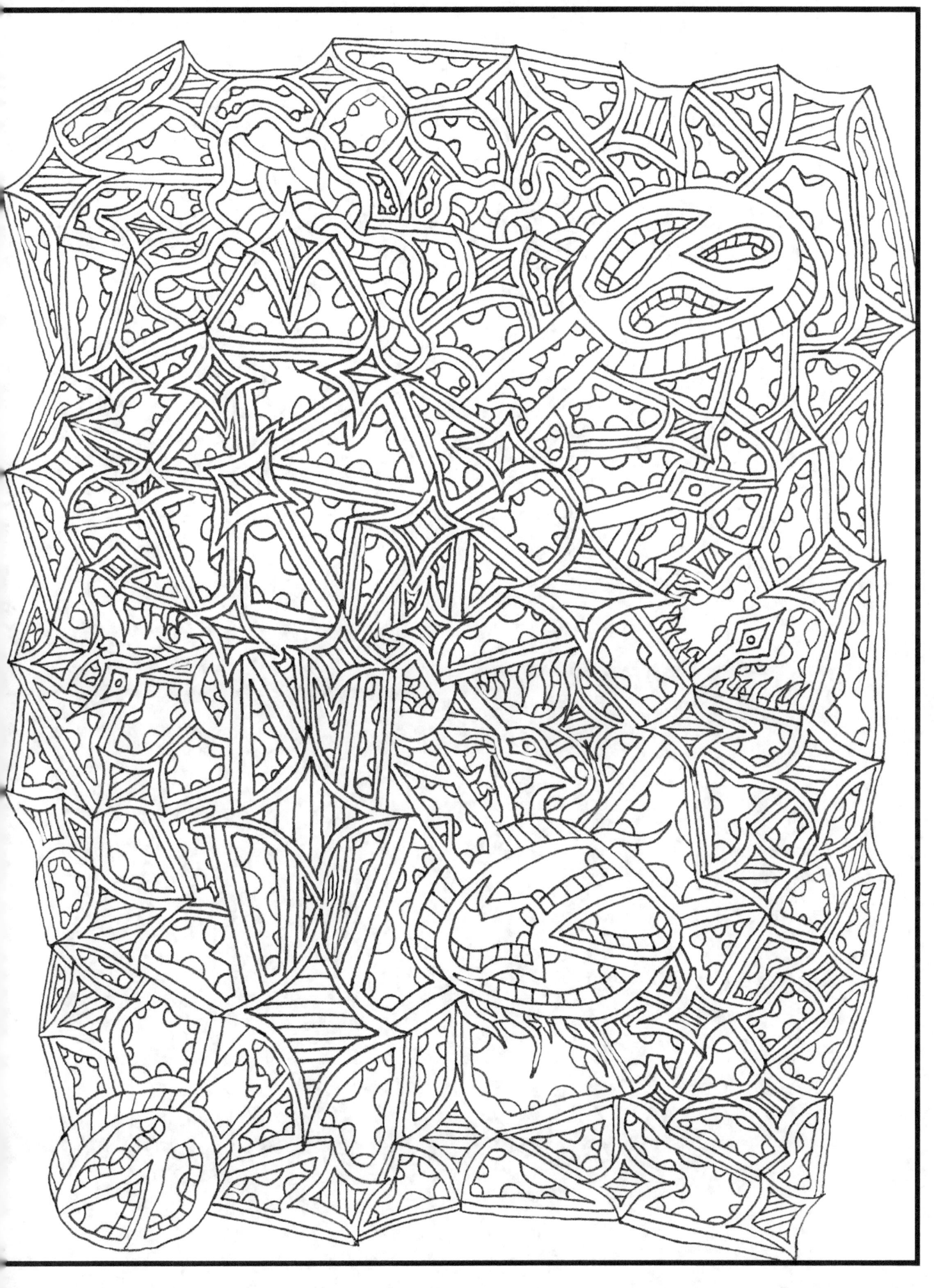

For more books
email me at damonehe@yahoo.com
or mail me at P.O. box
2433 Newport Oregon
97365
or you can visit damonesart.com

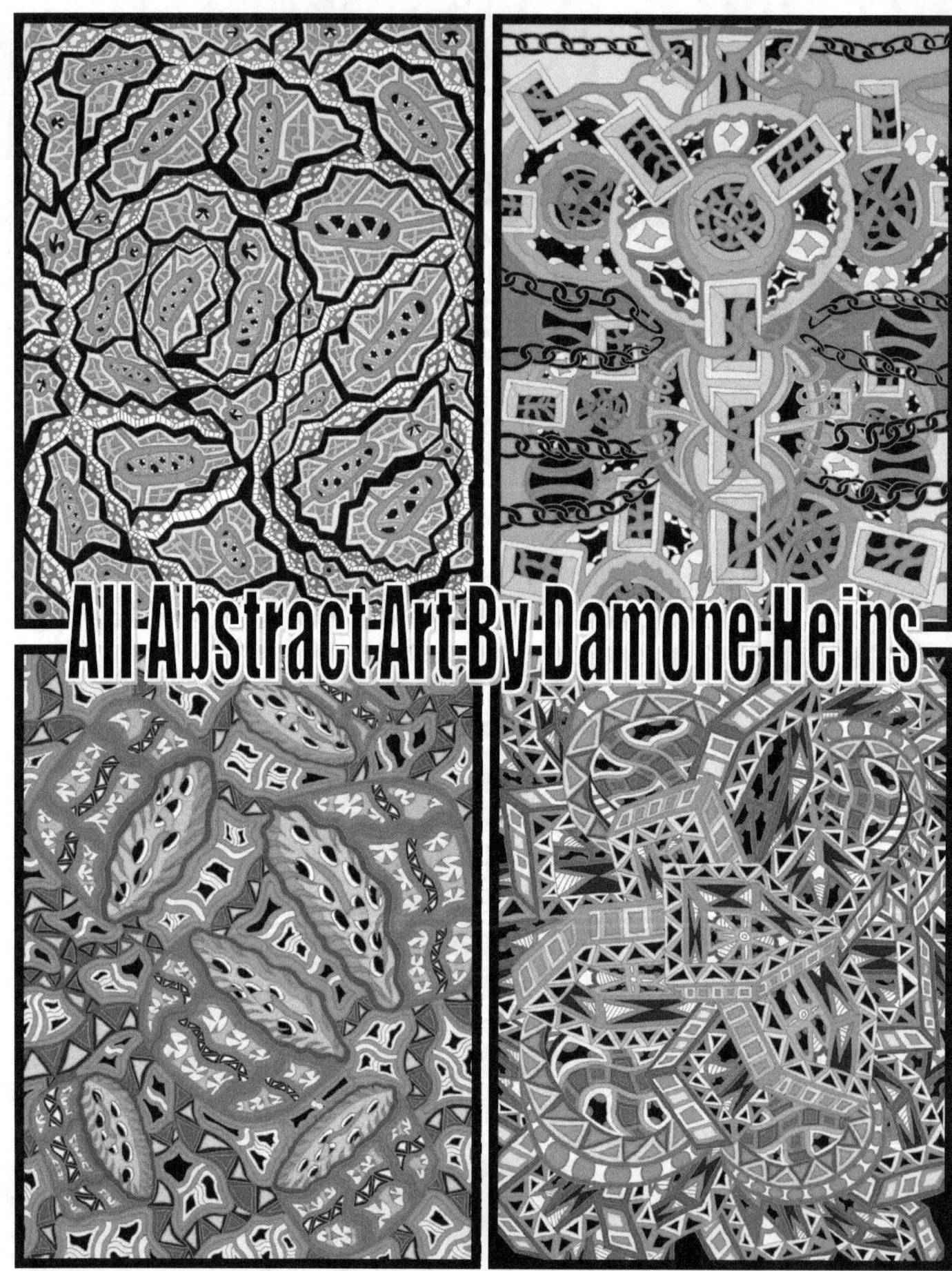

All Abstract Art By Damone Heins

www.ingramcontent.com/pod-product-compliance
Lightning Source LLC
Chambersburg PA
CBHW08201429O526
45787CB00016B/2800

* 9 7 8 1 5 3 3 1 0 6 2 6 1 *